Engineers can't write (and other witty poetry)

Eleanor Grey

BookLeaf Publishing

India | USA | UK

Presentation by *BookLeaf Publishing*

Web: www.bookleafpub.com

E-mail: info@bookleafpub.com

ISBN: 9789358312980

First edition 2023

For SJ, without your enthusiasm I would not have survived uni to this point, much less written this book

PREFACE

They say write about what you know. As an engineer, I de-stress by writing. A friend of mine talked me into compiling the poems I'd written about our engineering experiences. I obliged.

Engineers can't write

Engineers can't write
It's very clear to ~~sea~~ see
They're gifted brains just seem to be
Incapable of vocablary

They und3rstand big words
Like thermodynamics
Yet try to put it in a thesis
And easily it all falls to peices

They are grate with numbers
And alg3bra they excel at
Using letters is so easy
When, they have value numerically

But they cannot, form a sentence
Nay a phrase is just a struggle
And English students ~~grave~~ grieve
When they read there dessertations

A rhyme is challenging too
Which is why I writ this p0em
To prove that engineers can write
But guess I gave myself a fright

Because I can't.

The attire of an engineer

They say dress for the career you want
Not the career you possess
For the soul of man is laid to bear
By means of fancy dress

It seems to engineers at least
This memo was not passed on
Or else all engineers desire
To dress like fashionless morons

Forgive me for my slight critique
But you all have no sense of style
I appreciate the practicality
But why does it have to look so vile?

A tasteless hoodie for at home
Cargo pants to store all manner
Of things, like string and bolts
And every size of tiny spanner

And then for work? A pale blue shirt
The same blue every single day
Like you're back at school, back with the lads
All matching in every single way

The boiler suits I'll grant have use
As do the stained black steel cap boots
I'd just prefer it if you didn't need
To all wear the same flipping suits

So when you go to dress for work
Or come home after a long day
Just remember you're an engineer
But that doesn't mean you must dress that way!

Dating an engineer

To date an engineer is a struggle
We find it hard to chat and to mingle
You can't bear to be wrong
So arguments go on long
Which is why engineers tend to be single

Dear Mr Academic

Dear Mr Academic
I just have a few complaints
For your teaching assumes that
We are all engineering saints

We don't read extra textbooks
We don't pre-read all the slides
If we make it to your lecture
Know we've not purchased the guides

All our brains don't operate
On the same high plane as yours
So when you talk a bit too fast
We start seeking the doors

If you pause and ask a question
We will hang our heads in shame
For no one did the research
Or can join in your 'fun' game

We want to learn we really do
And apply it to our work
So please slow down and do not frown
When all we do is smirk

The engineering hierarchy

First the Aero-Astro lot
For their heads are in the sky
Then the Mech Eng motley crew
Whose broad knowledge gets them by

Next come the electrical
Dark magic is their science
Followed by acoustical
Who prefer to have silence

Biomed excel in aide
Of those with broken bodies
Nuclear play with atoms
Thus unlocking energy

Ship scientists have some use
Keeping our boats from breaking
Civil are just architects
That stop our bridges quaking

The innerworkings of the engineering mind

For Tom

That makes no sense
Why won't he fix it?
That hasn't reached
Elastic limit

They're just so wrong
They're simply blind
A double hinge's
What I have in mind

Remove that part
That isn't straight
Don't touch that thing
I need it's weight

That tool is mine
You use it wrong
My maths says this
It should be long

You've good intent
But lack all skill

Just leave me be
And pass the drill

Who designed this?
It's catastrophic
That person was
Devoid of logic

How lucky that
You have got me
An engineer
With eyes to see

That's no problem
I can solve this
To fix this issue
Brings me bliss

Engineering code

I understand (I really don't
Comprehend how you are just so
Blind to the truth, ignorant of
Life that you think this would work).

Let's try this (because your idea
while adorable just wouldn't
Cut the mustard, solve the problem,
Might even make it worsen).

I can manage (you really can't
Be trusted anywhere near this
Project, a liability
I can't think around, need my space).

Have you checked your maths (I just did
And unless you're planning to make
This for a mouse you really need
To fix this or I will have to).

I'm not quite sure (you're completely
Utterly inescapably
Wrong. I am certainly right for
My brain is just superior).

That's really great well done (you have
Exceeded expectations that
Were not that high to start with but
Nevertheless I'm still impressed).

What have I got in my pockets

A piece of string for calculating
circumferences of useful round things
Like barrels, or the span of a wing
Of a bird, not of a plane

A small screwdriver set, not just one
Otherwise nothing can be done
When faced with flat heads and everyone
Of your screwdrivers are Phillips

A Swiss Army knife, don't be obtuse
A tiny saw might come in use
To cut a twig, or else produce
A bottle opener to let liquid loose

A tape measure, a hammer too
Collection of mismatching screws
A USB, folding spoon, one or two
Buttons, threads of different shades of blue

And finally a broken doorbell
I said I'd fix three years ago, well
That hasn't happened and who can tell
When it will, so in my pocket it dwells.

When it shouldn't move

When securing a piece to another
It often can be quite a bother
But if something is loose
Or shouldn't move when in use
Some duck tape you should introduce

It should move

13

When moving a gear is unfruitful
And the package for grease is untruthful
To deal with the friction
And your current affliction
Turn to WD40, It's useful!

Why you need the engineer

Engineers made everything
That was not designed by God
This is not appreciated
As most don't give a sod

Where would you be without us
Couldn't get from a to b
No cars, no bikes, no trains, no planes
Just walking, don't you see?

And walk with what, your fancy shoes
Made by machines my man
Or else by fancy craftsmen
Part of the engineering clan

No computers, no roads, no bridges
No cameras, no electricity
No skyscrapers, no television
No phone, no life, no dignity

You'd have no food because we chose
To mechanise all farming
And hospitals without our help
Would be rather alarming

Without us life would be so dull
And you wouldn't have the means,
So you can do the things you want
We work hard behind the scenes

So next time you see an engineer
Thank them for all their service
In making and inventing stuff
For a greater purpose

This is a hammer

This is a hammer, use it to hit nails
This is a screwdriver, it screws in screws
A hammer is just not a screwdriver
Is this something you just never knew?
Or do you assume the thread is just
There to give you extra grip, as you hit
The screw into the wood at full force,
While the bag of nails sits full, you commit
The worst crime conceived, using the wrong tool
To do a job it wasn't designed to you fool!

Corrosion

For my supervisor

In the realm of metals, a subtle decay,
Corrosion emerges in diverse display.
Uniform attack, a silent invasion,
Metal's demise, a chemical persuasion.

Galvanic dance, where pairs intertwine,
Anodic sacrifice, cathodic design.
Metals in union, a current flows,
Corrosive tango, nature's tale it sows.

Pitting, a whisper, a localized strife,
Tiny craters form, consuming life.
In the sea's embrace or industrial strife,
Pits emerge, the silent corrosion knife.

Crevice corrosion, in shadows it creeps,
Hidden realms where corrosion seeps.
Cracks and corners, a clandestine play,
Metal's demise in a covert ballet.

Stress corrosion, under tension's grip,
Metal bows to the forces that strip.
A marriage of stress and corrosive art,

A slow, relentless, internal heart.

Atmospheric corrosion, the open air's kiss,
Oxidation's embrace, relentless abyss.
Rust's red touch, a visible plea,
Nature's claim on metal's decree.

Corrosion's tapestry, a tale diverse,
Metals succumb, their fate rehearse.
Yet in understanding, in science's light,
We seek to shield, to win the fight.

Marconium

19

For my dad

Marconium is wonderful, it's true
It's incredibly strong, who knew?
A versatile ace,
No limits to trace,
All engineering feats, it breaks through!

The engineering alphabet

A is for automotive, the engines' artistry,
Vehicles in motion, a marvel of machinery.

B is for biomimicry, nature's design to borrow,
Mirroring life's brilliance, innovation we follow.

C is for corrosion, disaster when it comes,
Draining life of metals, rust's silent drums.

D is for dynamics, investigating forces,
Manipulating movement, finding where
motion's source is.

E is for engineering, what else would I choose,
The discipline of kings, where innovation
ensues.

F is for fluids, important to understand,
Exerting different pressures on air, sea and land.

G is for gears, foundational to industry,
A rhythmic symphony, turning endlessly

H is for hydraulics, elevating heavy weights,
Utilising liquid, to lift big things on crates.

I is for isothermal, keeping constant heat,
Energy efficiency is its greatest feat.

J is for jig, mechanical support,
Workshop staple, stopping parts contort.

K is for kinetics, motion's detailed tale,
Energy in transit, a dynamic trail.

L is for lasers, used in additive manufacture,
Selectively melting, impacting microstructure.

M is for machining, frequently enjoyed,
Using exciting tools, or robots are deployed.

N is for nanotech, on a microscopic quest,
Manipulating matter, innovation at its best.

O is for oil, reducing friction,
Slick and smooth, a useful addition.

P is for phase diagram, understanding composition
Of composites and alloys, aiding material decision.

Q is for quality, for it we all strive,

It's why we are perfectionists, so engineering
thrives.

R is for robotics, electronic mystery,
Making mechanical friends, futuristic wizardry.

S is for sustainability, a vital decree,
Innovation for earth, our shared legacy.

T is for thermodynamics, heat's subtle play
In engines and systems, pretty graphs you can
display.

U is for ultrasonic, acoustical delight
Frequency unheard by man, yet gives useful
insight.

V is for vibrations, a rhythmic sensation,
Structural analysis, a critical foundation.

W is for welding, metals uniting,
In sparks and heat, craftsmanship igniting.

X is for xerography, a copying art,
In the reproduction world, where copies impart.

Y is for yield strength, material's might
Beyond it is failure, the engineer's fright.

Z is for zeppelin, soaring the sky,
An engineering marvel, floating up high.

Why cars are better than planes

I do not doubt that some may say
Planes beat cars in every way.
They the great engineering feat,
Not bound by carriageway or street.

Planes may soar in skies so vast,
But cars connect, a bond that lasts.
Winding paths, beneath the sun,
Adventures shared, one by one.

No boarding passes, no delays,
Just open roads, in endless ways.
The joy of driving, windows down,
Chasing horizons, town to town.

The bond you form with your dear car
Beats any flight from near to far,
So you may fly across the sea,
I will drive the car so dear to me.

The boy stood on the burning deck

The boy stood on the burning deck
A blow torch in his hand.
Feeling quite sick,
Realised he's thick,
And should really weld on land.

Women in STEM

You are so brave, you are so strong,
You simply can't do any wrong
So speaks the feminist to me,
The Queen to the worker bee,
So strong is the woman in STEM.

As if this choice of career was
A burden, chosen for the cause
of equal rights, and equal pay,
So patriarchy goes away,
So chooses the woman in STEM.

The world forgets the way our mind
Is wired, machines of every kind
Adored, previously unseen
By female peers who were once mean
To the poor women in STEM.

Teased for nerdy interests, yet
Now wheeled out to represent, bet
Our useful femininity
Lead to responsibility,
So used are the women in STEM.

Look at us now, who overcame

Not men but women, playing games
That caused us pain, you want us now,
To represent, so you must bow
Bow before the women in STEM.

Engineering humour

The engineer's humour is dark,
For self deprivation's a lark.
Our job's so hard you see
So it doesn't break me
To use jokes beats an honest remark!

A love letter to the internal combustion engine

In the heart of steel, a rhythmic beat,
Engines hum, a melody sweet.
Pistons dance in precision's trance,
A symphony of power, a mechanic's romance.

Fuel coursing veins of intricate design,
Igniting dreams, the automotive shrine.
Gears interlock, a seamless ballet,
In the language of motion, they silently say.

Chrome and steel, a polished sheen,
A roaring force, a mechanical queen.
Turbo whispers, a breath of might,
Engines pulsating, in the realm of flight.

From the purr of a kitten to a lion's roar,
A tapestry woven, power to explore.
Oil-stained hands, a craftsman's art,
In the world of engines, a beating heart.

Why I wrote this book

To study engineering is great,
But the work really isn't first-rate.
With lab work so tough,
And assignments so rough,
It's much more fun to procrastinate!

www.ingramcontent.com/pod-product-compliance
Lightning Source LLC
LaVergne TN
LVHW010949200726
843509LV00013B/2335